AN EVALUATION PRIMER WORKBOOK:

PRACTICAL EXERCISES FOR EDUCATORS

by Arlene Fink and Jacqueline Kosecoff

SAGE PUBLICATIONS   Beverly Hills   London

© 1978 by Arlene Fink and Jacqueline Kosecoff

For information address:

SAGE Publications, Inc.
275 South Beverly Drive
Beverly Hills, California 90212

SAGE Publications, Ltd
28 Banner Street
London EC1Y 8QE, England

Printed in the United States of America

ISBN 0-8039-1481-4
Library of Congress Catalog Card Number 77-088462

THIRD PRINTING

INTRODUCTION

This workbook is designed to be used with *An Evaluation Primer* by Arlene Fink and Jacqueline Kosecoff. The exercises included here are intended to provide practice in applying evaluation skills to education programs. Each chapter in this workbook corresponds to a chapter in *An Evaluation Primer*.

TABLE OF CONTENTS

CHAPTER 1
AN INTRODUCTION TO EVALUATION

EXERCISE 1-A:
IDENTIFYING THE CONTEXT OF AN EVALUATION

Directions:

Decide whether each of the following evaluations is being performed in an improvement or an effectiveness context and justify your choice. The answers to this exercise can be found on page 5.

Evaluation #1 Ellenborough Elementary School's reading program for gifted children is in its second year. An evaluation will be conducted to find out whether all students in the program have access to the books they need and whether teachers were trained to work with gifted children. The information will be used by the program staff to continue development of curriculum materials and inservice training.

Context _____ Improvement _____ Effectiveness

Justification

Evaluation #2 Johnson School District has commissioned an evaluation to determine which of two vocational education programs better prepares its students for jobs. Based on the evaluation's findings, one of the programs will be adopted for district-wide use.

Context _____ Improvement _____ Effectiveness

Justification

Evaluation #3 The National Office of Educational Quality is conducting an evaluation of its ten-year-old compensatory education program. The evaluation will produce information about the number and characteristics of students participating in the program and the nature of the services provided to them. The evaluation information will be used to determine if modifications are needed and, if so, in what areas.

Context　　　_____ Improvement　　　_____ Effectiveness

Justification

Evaluation #4 Johnson Junior High School has begun a program to train handicapped students to acquire basic office skills. The federal agency that sponsors the program requires an evaluation report at the end of the first year to be used as a basis for refunding and continuation decisions.

Context　　　_____ Improvement　　　_____ Effectiveness

Justification

EXERCISE 1-B:
SELECTING AN EVALUATOR

Directions:

Below is a description of a program, its evaluation requirements, and excerpts from the resumés of three applicants for the job of evaluator. Select the *one* applicant who best fits the described position and justify your decision. You should also justify your rejection of the other two applicants. The answers to this exercise can be found on page 6.

Program Description
Co-op Village is a state-funded apartment community for low- to middle-income families who have been uprooted from their homes by urban renewal or highway construction.

Evaluation Requirements
State sponsors have called for an evaluation to improve this developing program. The evaluation is to answer questions such as these: "Do residents like the park and recreational facilities?" "Are facilities such as heating and air conditioning adequate?" The evaluator will be expected to work with state and city representatives and residents to refine the evaluation questions. The job will require the evaluator to design questionnaires, conduct surveys, and analyze and report the results.

RESUMÉ EXCERPTS

Applicant	Resumé Excerpt	Applicant Selected/ Rejected and Justification
S. Greenfield	*Education:* 1960, B.A., English, Marquette University 1965, Ph.D., Psychology, University of Southern California *Skills:* Principal components analysis; varimax rotation factor analysis; multivariate analysis of co-variance structures; cognitive and affective test development *Experience:* Test selection consultant to L.O. City Housing Cooperative; psychometric consultant to Abiquet, New Mexico to design housing survey instruments; consultant to E.S.Q., Inc. in data analysis and reporting; consultant to UCSDL in the design and validation of survey instruments *No. of Publications:* 15 *Sample Publications:* Greenfield, S. "The Multidimensional Scaling of Survey Measures." *Multivariate Performance Research*, 1975, 2, 453-459. Greenfield, S. "Using Multiple Moderators in Prediction." *Journal of Vocational Measurement*, 1976, 3, 101-107.	
Betty Gold	*Education:* 1963, B.A., Psychology, Barnard College 1969, M.A., Research Methods, UCLA *Skills:* Research design and data analysis; instrument development for evaluation surveys including questionnaires and measures of achievement and attitude *Experience:* Research associate for an evaluation of the Illinois statewide urban renewal program; senior staff member of Richard School District's survey research and evaluation group; evaluator for Lockhugh Inc.'s vocational training program	

Applicant	Resumé Excerpt	Applicant Selected/ Rejected and Justification
Betty Gold (continued)	*No. of Publications:* 7 *Sample Publications:* Gold, B. "An Evaluation of a State-wide Program," *Evaluator*, 1975, 2-9. Gold, B. "The Politics of Evaluation: Title XXXI." *American Social Science*, 1976, 3, 303-309.	
R. Brook	*Education:* 1959, B.A., Mathematics, Harvard University 1963, M.S., Computer Science, Michigan State University *Skills:* Computer programming in ALGOL, COBOL, PL1; statistical analysis including regression techniques, multivariate analysis of covariance, factor analysis, and non-parametric procedures *Experience:* Lecturer in mathematics at Michigan University; consultant to the Associate Director of HVM for research design; consultant to Ultratech Inc. in instrument design *No. of Publications:* 11 *Sample Publications:* Brook, R. "Problems in the Application of Cross-Lagged Panel Correlations." Paper presented to the American Evaluation Research Association, Paris, April, 1975. Brook, R. "A Covariance Structure Model for Community Data." *Issues in Evaluation*, 1976, 5, 402-405.	

Answers to Exercise 1-A: Identifying the Context of an Evaluation

Evaluation #1 Ellenborough Elementary School's reading program for gifted children is in its second year. An evaluation will be conducted to find out whether all students in the program have access to the books they need and whether teachers were trained to work with gifted children. The information will be used by the program staff to continue development of curriculum materials and inservice training.

Context   ✓ Improvement   _____ Effectiveness

Justification *The evaluation is being conducted in an improvement context because its information will be used to assist program development.*

Evaluation #2 Johnson School District has commissioned an evaluation to determine which of two vocational education programs better prepares its students for jobs. Based on the evaluation's findings, one of the programs will be adopted for district-wide use.

Context   _____ Improvement   ✓ Effectiveness

Justification *The evaluation is being conducted in an effectiveness context because its information will be used to certify a program.*

Evaluation #3 The National Office of Educational Quality is conducting an evaluation of its ten-year-old compensatory education program. The evaluation will produce information about the number and characteristics of students participating in the program and the nature of the services provided to them. The evaluation information will be used to determine if modifications are needed and, if so, in what areas.

Context   ✓ Improvement   _____ Effectiveness

Justification *The evaluation is being conducted in an improvement context because its information will be used to decide whether changes are needed to improve the program.*

Evaluation #4 Johnson Junior High School has begun a program to train handicapped students to acquire basic office skills. The federal agency that sponsors the program requires an evaluation report at the end of the first year to be used as a basis for refunding and continuation decisions.

Context   _____ Improvement   ✓ Effectiveness

Justification *The evaluation is being conducted in an effectiveness context because its information will be used to decide whether the program deserves to be refunded.*

Answers to Exercise 1-B: Selecting an Evaluator

Applicant	Resumé Excerpt	Applicant Selected/Rejected and Justification
S. Greenfield	*Education:* 1960, B.A., English, Marquette University 1965, Ph.D., Psychology, University of Southern California *Skills:* Principal components analysis; varimax rotation factor analysis; multivariate analysis of covariance structures; cognitive and affective test development *Experience:* Test selection consultant to L.O. City Housing Cooperative; psychometric consultant to Abiquet, New Mexico to design housing survey instruments; consultant to E.S.Q. Inc. in data analysis and reporting; consultant to UCSDL in the design and validation of survey instruments *No. of Publications:* 15 *Sample Publications:* Greenfield, S. "The Multidimensional Scaling of Survey Measures." *Multivariate Performance Research,* 1975, 2, 453-459. Greenfield, S. "Using Multiple Moderators in Prediction." *Journal of Vocational Measurement,* 1976, 3, 101-107.	*We would reject Dr. Greenfield because although he seems to be an excellent psychometrician, he lacks evaluation experience. He is our second choice, however, because he has experience designing and validating instruments and working with housing programs.*
Betty Gold	*Education:* 1963, B.A., Psychology, Barnard College 1969, M.A., Research Methods, UCLA *Skills:* Research design and data analysis; instrument development for evaluation surveys including questionnaires and measures of achievement and attitude *Experience:* Research associate for an evaluation of the Illinois statewide urban renewal program; senior staff member of Richard School	*We would select Ms. Gold because she has been trained in evaluation, has had experience conducting evaluation studies, and has worked on a major urban renewal project. In addition, she has some instrument development, data analysis, and reporting skills.*

Applicant	Resumé Excerpt	Applicant Selected/ Rejected and Justification
	District's survey research and evaluation group; evaluator for Lockhugh Inc.'s vocational training program *No. of Publications:* 7 *Sample Publications:* Gold, B. "An Evaluation of a State-wide Program." *Evaluator*, 1975, 2-9. Gold, B. "The Politics of Evaluation: Title XXXI." *American Social Science*, 1976, 3, 303-309.	
R. Brook	*Education:* 1959, B.A. Mathematics, Harvard University 1963, M.S., Computer Science, Michigan State University *Skills:* Computer programming in ALGOL, COBOL, PL1; statistical analysis including regression techniques, multivariate analysis of co-variance, factor analysis, and non-parametric procedures *Experience:* Lecturer in mathematics at Michigan University; consultant to the Associate Director of HVM for research design; consultant to Ultratech Inc. in instrument design *No. of Publications:* 11 *Sample Publications:* Brook, R. "Problems in the Application of Cross-Lagged Panel Correlations." Paper presented to the American Evaluation Research Association, Paris, April, 1975. Brook, R. "A Covariance Structure Model for Community Data." *Issues in Evaluation*, 1976, 5, 402-405.	*We would reject Mr. Brook. He has very specialized mathematics and computer programming skills that may be useful, but has no experience in conducting evaluations, working with housing programs, and developing instruments.*

CHAPTER 2
FORMULATING CREDIBLE EVALUATION QUESTIONS

EXERCISE 2-A:
DESIGNING AN EVALUATOR'S
PROGRAM DESCRIPTION

Directions:

In this three-part exercise, you will complete portions of an Evaluator's Program Description (EPD). For each part of the exercise, you will be given excerpts from a dialogue among the evaluator, the project director, and the curriculum consultant, as well as a partially-completed portion of the EPD. Use the information in the dialogue to complete the unfinished portions of the EPD.

Each part of the exercise refers to an improvement evaluation for a compensatory education program designed to teach reading and mathematics to high school students in a correctional institution. The answers to this exercise can be found on page 13.

PART I

Fill in the missing information after reading the dialogue below.

Goals	Activities	Evidence of Program Merit
1. _____ _____ _____ _____ _____ _____	_____ _____ _____ _____ _____ _____ _____	_____ _____ _____

DIALOGUE

Evaluator: As you know, the purpose of this meeting is to create the Evaluator's Program Description. Let's begin with my telling you what I know about the general purpose of your program. It is designed for neglected and delinquent youth and is funded under Title I, ESEA.

Project Director: Let me interrupt you to state more specifically some of our goals and activities. One of our major objectives is to have students use materials like job advertisements and applications, driver's tests, and directions for using household products.

Evaluator: Why are you doing this?

Curriculum Consultant: We have found that our students learn best through direct practice, so we use curriculum materials that give many opportunities to read street signs, brand names, etc. We think this will help students acquire skills needed for everyday reading.

Evaluator: Oh, so providing students with a set of minimum reading skills is your goal, and using curriculum materials that are a part of everyday experience is an activity to achieve that goal.

Curriculum Consultant: Yes. In addition to using these curriculum materials, another activity for this goal is having students watch the educational television station's reading show.

Evaluator: How will you know if students have acquired everyday reading skills?

Project Director: We have a performance test that measures how well students can read labels, directions, applications, etc. In the past, about 60% of our students performed satisfactorily on the test. According to our reading consultant, an 8% increase would be an educationally significant gain.

Evaluator: Shall I also report on whether students actually use the curriculum materials and watch educational television as planned?

Project Director: No. We don't really need that information right now ...

PART II

Fill in the missing information after reading the dialogue below.

Goals	Activities	Evidence of Program Merit
------------------------	------------------------	------------------------
------------------------	------------------------	------------------------
------------------------	------------------------	------------------------
------------------------		
------------------------		------------------------
------------------------		------------------------

DIALOGUE

Evaluator: What other goals does the program have?

Curriculum Consultant: Another major goal is to provide students with the skills needed for everyday mathematics. To do this, students are given practice computing bills and interest and making budgets.

Evaluator: How will you know whether or not this has been achieved?

Project Director: We will consider the program successful if students significantly improve their math skills from the beginning to the end of the program.

Evaluator: Are you also concerned about whether the instruction really gives students practice computing bills and so on?

Project Director: Yes. Without this kind of practice, we will not consider our program a success.

PART III

Fill in the missing information after reading the dialogue below.

Goals	Activities	Evidence of Program Merit
3. _____ _____ _____ _____ _____ _____	_____ _____ _____	_____ _____ _____ _____ _____ _____ _____

DIALOGUE

Evaluator: Are there any other goals?

Project Director: No.

Curriculum Consultant: No.

Evaluator: But the state guidelines for this program require that an affective component be included in each program.

Project Director: Oh yes. We have an affective goal, "to increase students' confidence in their everyday reading and mathematics abilities."

Curriculum Consultant: To meet this goal, we have used John Doe's research that indicates compensatory students often learn best in small groups and at their own rate. We have organized our classrooms to conform to this finding.

Project Director: To be sure we've accomplished this goal, we will interview our students to find out how they feel and survey our teachers ...

EXERCISE 2-B:
WRITING EVALUATION QUESTIONS

Directions:

Using the answers to Exercise 2-A, the completed EPD for the compensatory education program for institutionalized students, write eight evaluation questions. Five questions should be directly based on the EPD and three should be based on other considerations. The answers to this exercise are on page 14.

EVALUATION QUESTIONS

Questions based on the EPD

1. _____
   _____?

2. _____
   _____?

3. _____
   _____?

4. _____
   _____?

5. _____
   _____?

Some questions not specifically based on the EPD

1. _____
   _____?

2. _____
   _____?

3. _____
   _____?

Answers to Exercise 2-A:
Designing an Evaluator's Program Description

	Goals	Activities	Evidence of Program Merit
P A R T I	1. To provide students with a set of minimum reading skills	• Using curriculum materials that are part of everyday experience (e.g. job application forms, driver's test) • Having students watch the educational television station	• At least 68% of the students demonstrate satisfactory reading skills
P A R T II	2. To provide students with the skills needed for everyday mathematics	• Students are given practice computing bills and interest and making budgets	• The occurrence of practice involving bills, interest, and budgets • A significant increase in students' math skills from the beginning to the end of the program
P A R T III	3. To increase students' confidence in their everyday reading and mathematics abilities	• Students learn in small groups and at their own rate	• Testimony from students that they are more confident • Testimony from teachers that students are more confident

Answers to Exercise 2-B: Writing Evaluation Questions

Questions based on the EPD

1. *Did at least 68% of the students demonstrate satisfactory reading skills?*

2. *Did students practice computing bills and interest and making budgets?*

3. *Did students' math skills increase significantly from the beginning to the end of the program?*

4. *Did students report that they are more confident of their ability to do everyday reading and mathematics?*

5. *Did teachers report that students are more confident of their ability to do everyday reading and mathematics?*

Questions not specifically based on the EPD

1. *Which students benefit most from the program?*

2. *How do the activities and outcomes of this program compare with other programs funded by Title I for students in correctional institutions?*

3. *What will be the benefits of a 10% per pupil increase in program funds?*

CHAPTER 3
CONSTRUCTING
EVALUATION DESIGNS

EXERCISE 3-A:
IDENTIFYING EVALUATION DESIGN STRATEGIES

Directions:

Based on a brief description of an evaluation, decide whether a case, time series, or comparison group design strategy is being used. The answers to this exercise are on page 19.

Evaluation Design Strategy	Case	Time Series	Comparison Group
1. To evaluate our program, we measure students' scores at the end of the year against the national norms.			
2. At the end of the year, all students in the program take a test, and their teachers complete a questionnaire.			
3. Throughout the nation, students are observed at the beginning of the program, immediately after the program, and six months after the program.			

EXERCISE 3-B:
FINDING INDEPENDENT AND DEPENDENT VARIABLES IN EVALUATION QUESTIONS

Directions:

For each evaluation question, find the independent and dependent variables. The answers to this exercise are on page 20.

Evaluation Question   1. At what level of schooling (i.e., elementary, secondary, and post secondary) were the participants most satisfied with the program?

Independent Variable(s)

Dependent Variable(s)

Evaluation Question   2. What effect do the PEP program and the ACT program have on the physical fitness of students who participate for half an hour and for one hour each day?

Independent Variable(s)

Dependent Variable(s)

Evaluation Question   3. How do Programs A and B compare in their impact on participants' self concept and motivation?

Independent Variable(s)

Dependent Variable(s)

EXERCISE 3-C:
ILLUSTRATING EVALUATION DESIGN STRATEGIES

Directions:

Based on a brief description of an evaluation, draw a picture to illustrate the design strategy being used. The answers to this exercise are on page 21.

Evaluation Description	Illustration
1. The purposes of the evaluation are to determine which of three bilingual programs is most effective and whether effectiveness is related to teachers' racial/ethnic backgrounds.	
2. The evaluation of Program LEARN will produce information about the characteristics of successful teachers who are also principals. This will require the evaluator to visit the school district one day a week for 14 weeks.	

EXERCISE 3-D:
DETERMINING THREATS TO INTERNAL AND EXTERNAL VALIDITY

Directions:

Look at the following list of possible threats to internal and external validity and decide whether each is a realistic threat in an evaluation of two elementary school programs for children with special learning disabilities. Both programs are meant to improve students' basic skills. The evaluation will focus on how well each program accomplishes that goal. Both programs will use the same achievement test administered at the beginning and end of the school year. Parents can choose either program for their eligible children. The evaluation's design strategy can be depicted as:

	Program 1	Program 2
Pretest		
Posttest		

The answers to this exercise are on page 21.

		Is this a threat?		Your Explanation
		Yes	No	
Threats to Internal Validity	History			
	Maturation			
	Testing			
	Instrumentation			
	Statistical Regression			
	Selection			
	Mortality			

		Is this a threat?		Your Explanation
		Yes	No	
Threats to External Validity	Reactive Effects of Testing			
	Interactive Effects of Selection Bias			
	Reactive Effects of Innovation			
	Multiple Program Interference			

Answers to Exercise 3-A:
Identifying Evaluation Design Strategies

Evaluation Design Strategy	Case	Time Series	Comparison Group
1. To evaluate our program, we measure students' scores at the end of the year against the national norms.			√
2. At the end of the year, all students in the program take a test, and their teachers complete a questionnaire.	√		
3. Throughout the nation, students are observed at the beginning of the program, immediately after the program, and six months after the program.		√	

Answers to Exercise 3-B:
Finding Independent and Dependent Variables in Evaluation Questions

Evaluation Question	1. At what level of schooling (i.e., elementary, secondary, and post secondary) were the participants most satisfied with the program?
Independent Variable(s)	*Level of schooling (which is being studied at three levels: elementary, secondary, and post secondary)*
Dependent Variable(s)	*Satisfaction with the program*

Evaluation Question	2. What effect do the PEP program and the ACT program have on the physical fitness of students who participate for half an hour and for one hour each day?
Independent Variable(s)	*Program participation (which is being studied at two levels: PEP and ACT)* *Time spent in physical education (which is being studied at two levels: half an hour and a hour per day)*
Dependent Variable(s)	*Physical fitness*

Evaluation Question	3. How do Programs A and B compare in their impact on participants' self concept and motivation?
Independent Variable(s)	*Program participation (which is being studied at two levels: Program A and Program B)*
Dependent Variable(s)	*Self concept* *Motivation*

Answers to Exercise 3-C:
Illustrating Evaluation Design Strategies

Evaluation Description	Illustration

1. The purposes of the evaluation are to determine which of three bilingual programs is most effective and whether effectiveness is related to teachers' racial/ethnic backgrounds.

	Program 1	Program 2	Program 3
Anglo Teachers			
Spanish Heritage Teachers			
Black Teachers			
Asian Teachers			
Other			

2. The evaluation of Program LEARN will produce information about the characteristics of successful teachers who are also principals. This will require the evaluator to visit the school district one day a week for 14 weeks.

Program LEARN

Answers to Exercise 3-D:
Determining Threats to Internal and External Validity

		Is this a threat? Yes	Is this a threat? No	Your Explanation
Threats to Internal Validity	History		✓	Students in both programs would be influenced by a historical event
	Maturation		✓	Students in both programs will mature
	Testing		✓	Any effects that taking a pretest would have on posttest results would occur in both programs
	Instrumentation		✓	Any calibration or test administration problems would affect participants in both programs
	Statistical Regression		✓	Program participants were not selected on the basis of their very high or very low scores
	Selection	✓		Parents whose children are relatively more disabled may systematically choose one of the programs; selection might interact with maturation, history, etc.
	Mortality		✓	If only those data from students who took the pretest and posttest are analyzed and interpreted, it would be possible to control for mortality
Threats to External Validity	Reactive Effects of Testing	✓		It is possible that the test in conjunction with one of the programs influenced students to improve their skills
	Interactive Effects of Selection Bias	✓		The evaluation findings cannot be generalized to other students with learning disabilities
	Reactive Effects of Innovation	✓		It is possible that students' excitement at participating in the program and evaluation influenced them to improve their skills
	Multiple Program Interference		✓	Not likely since no other concurrent program is mentioned

CHAPTER 4
PLANNING INFORMATION COLLECTION

EXERCISE 4-A:
SELECTING, ADAPTING, AND
DEVELOPING INSTRUMENTS

Directions:

In this exercise, you are asked to decide whether to select, adapt, or develop specific information collection instruments and to describe how you would go about preparing or obtaining the instruments. To do this, you are given titles of programs to be evaluated, a description of information collection techniques to be used in the evaluation of each program, and comments that will help you to make a decision. The answers to this exercise are on page 26.

Program #1: BILINGUAL EDUCATION

INFORMATION COLLECTION TECHNIQUES	Reading achievement test in Spanish and English; vocabulary test in Spanish and English
COMMENTS	The program staff has already developed a reading achievement test in Spanish only.
PROBLEM	Would you select, adapt, or develop instruments? Explain your choice.

Program #2: YOUTH JUSTICE VOCATIONAL INSTITUTE

INFORMATION COLLECTION TECHNIQUES	Interviews with former juvenile offenders and their employers
COMMENTS	The interviews should be informal but structured. This is a low-budget evaluation.
PROBLEM	Would you select, adapt, or develop instruments? Explain your choice.

Program #3: COMMUNITY LEARNING CENTER

INFORMATION COLLECTION TECHNIQUES	Questionnaire survey of community members
COMMENTS	The questionnaire will be sent to a random sample of registered voters in the community to see if they know about the center, how to make use of it, and whether they are using or intend to use it.
PROBLEM	Would you select, adapt, or develop instruments? Explain your choice.

Program #4: CAREER AWARENESS PROGRAM FOR ADULT WOMEN

INFORMATION COLLECTION TECHNIQUES	A career preference test given to participants at the beginning and end of the program
COMMENTS	The career preference test given at the beginning of the program is used to tailor course materials to participants' interests. The before- and after-training test results are used by the evaluator to measure changes in the participants' career interests.
PROBLEM	Would you select, adapt, or develop instruments? Explain your choice.

EXERCISE 4-B:
COMPLETING THE EVALUATION QUESTIONS
WITH INFORMATION COLLECTION TECHNIQUES

Directions:

Complete the missing parts of the EQ with ICT for an evaluation of the effectiveness of a new districtwide secretarial skills vocational education program. A comparison group design was used to compare the new secretarial skills program with the traditional one. For the evaluation, all participating high school students in the district were randomly assigned to one of the two programs. The answers to this exercise can be found on page 27.

Evaluation Questions With Information Collection Techniques:
Vocational Education Program

Evaluation Questions	Information Collection Techniques	Limitations			
		Schedule	Design	Sampling	Other
1. How successful was the new vocational program compared to the traditional program in improving students' secretarial skills?		A postmeasure must be administered in May.	Students in the new program may perform well because of their excitement at participating in an innovative class.	No sampling of vocational students in either program is permitted.	
2. Compared to the traditional program, how much did the new program affect participants' attitudes toward their academic courses?		Measures must be made at the end of each semester.	Teachers tend to give high evaluations to all students.		Must respect privacy laws.
3. To what extent did the new and traditional programs expand participants' career options?		A premeasure must be administered in September and a postmeasure can only be administered in May.	Transfer students may have participated in the program for just a few months.		

EXERCISE 4-C:
COMPLETING THE INFORMATION
COLLECTION PLAN

Directions:

Using as a guide the program described in Exercise 4-B and its EQ with ICT, complete the missing parts of the Information Collection Plan for the secretarial skills vocational educational program. The answers to this exercise are on page 28.

Information Collection Plan

Specific Information Collection Techniques	Times and Places for Information Collection	Nature of the Sample for the Technique	Who Will Collect the Information

Answers to Exercise 4-A:
Selecting, Adapting and Developing Instruments

Program #1: BILINGUAL EDUCATION

INFORMATION COLLECTION TECHNIQUES	Reading achievement test in Spanish and English; vocabulary test in Spanish and English
COMMENTS	The program staff has already developed a reading achievement test in Spanish only.
PROBLEM	Would you select, adapt, or develop instruments? Explain your choice. *You should use the program staff's reading test if it has been validated. If not, you might look for an already-validated Spanish reading test or validate theirs.* *You should select or adapt an English reading test and Spanish and English vocabulary tests.* *You should see if the tests you want to select or adapt require additional validation.*

Program #2: YOUTH JUSTICE VOCATIONAL INSTITUTE

INFORMATION COLLECTION TECHNIQUES	Interviews with former juvenile offenders and their employers
COMMENTS	The interviews should be informal but structured. This is a low-budget evaluation.
PROBLEM	Would you select, adapt, or develop instruments? Explain your choice. *You should probably develop an interview form since it is unlikely that one already exists for the specific purposes of this evaluation. Refer to previously used interview schedules, if they are available, to help you develop the interview form.*

Program #3: COMMUNITY LEARNING CENTER

INFORMATION COLLECTION TECHNIQUES	Questionnaire survey of community members
COMMENTS	The questionnaire will be sent to a random sample of registered voters in the community to see if they know about the center, how to make use of it, and whether they are using it or intend to use it.
PROBLEM	Would you select, adapt, or develop instruments? Explain your choice. *You would probably develop the questionnaire form. Other previously used questionnaires might be used as a reference guide to help structure and format the new questionnaire.*

Program #4: CAREER AWARENESS PROGRAM FOR ADULT WOMEN

INFORMATION COLLECTION TECHNIQUES	A career preference test given to participants at the beginning and end of the program
COMMENTS	The career preference test given at the beginning of the program is used to tailor course materials to participant's interests. The before- and after-training test results are used by the evaluator to measure changes in the participants' career interests.
PROBLEM	Would you select, adapt, or develop instruments? Explain your choice.
	You would probably select an already-developed and validated career preference test. Several such tests exist and are available from commercial publishers. Given the amount of time and money invested in commercial measures, it is doubtful that an evaluator with limited resources could develop a better test.
	You might have to pay special attention to validating the test to make sure that it is appropriate for adult women. Many career preference tests are biased towards men's career interests and experiences or towards younger adults' interests and opportunities.

Answers to Exercise 4-B:
Completing the Evaluation Questions with Information Collection Techniques

Evaluation Questions	Information Collection Techniques	Limitations			
		Schedule	Design	Sampling	
1. How successful was the new vocational program compared to the traditional program in improving students' secretarial skills?	*Standard performance test of secretarial skills*	A postmeasure must be administered in May.	Students in the new program may perform well because of their excitement at participating in an innovative class.	No sampling of vocational students in either program is permitted.	
2. Compared to the traditional program, how much did the new program affect participants' attitudes toward their academic courses?	*Review of students' grades in their academic courses* *Review of students' attendance records in their academic courses*	Measures must be made at the end of each semester.	Teachers tend to give high evaluations to all students.		Must respect privacy laws.
3. To what extent did the new and traditional programs expand participants' options?	*Student questionnaires*	A premeasure must be administered in September and a postmeasure can only be administered in May.	Transfer students may have participated in the program for just a few months.		

Answers to Exercise 4-C:
Completing the Information Collection Plan

Specific Information Collection Techniques	Times and Places for Information Collection	Nature of the Sample for the Technique	Who Will Collect the Information
The Sawyer Performance Test of Secretarial Skills	In May in students' classrooms	All students in the new and traditional vocational programs	The evaluation team will train teachers to administer the test
Review of students' grades in their academic courses	At the end of each semester in the administrative offices	All students in the new program and a random sample of 25% of the students in the traditional program	The evaluation team with the assistance of school personnel
Review of students' attendance records in their academic courses	At the end of each semester in the attendance office	All students in the new program and a random sample of 25% of the students in the traditional program	The evaluation team with assistance from school personnel
The Student Career Interest Questionnaire	In September and May in students' classrooms	All students in the new and traditional vocational programs	The evaluation team will train teachers to administer the tests

CHAPTER 5
COLLECTING EVALUATION INFORMATION

EXERCISE 5-A:
MEASUREMENT VALIDITY

Directions:

Select the major type of measurement validity that is emphasized in each of the following situations. Indicate your answer by circling the letter that corresponds to the appropriate kind of validity where:

A = Predictive validity
B = Concurrent validity
C = Content validity
D = Construct validity

The answers to this exercise can be found on page 33.

	Predictive	Concurrent	Content	Construct	
A	B	C	D		1. At the end of the second year of medical school, students take a battery of tests to find out who will and will not become good doctors.
A	B	C	D		2. Teacher's evaluation of the quality of student writing was correlated with scores obtained on the APC Test of Writing Ability.
A	B	C	D		3. Confronted by a frantic student who has just received the results of his/her History 103 test, the teacher discovers that the student in question was given a History 113 test by mistake.
A	B	C	D		4. The director of the Center for the Study of Instruction judges which teachers will benefit from the workshop on how to evaluate educational materials.
A	B	C	D		5. Teachers who become angry in an experimental situation also obtain higher anger scores on the new personality measure than do teachers whose anger is not experimentally manipulated.
A	B	C	D		6. Confident that the professor has not changed his course, students studied for the final exam by reviewing their fraternity's file of past exams.
A	B	C	D		7. A diagnosis of brain damage based on the new XYZ Perceptual Performance Test is compared with the results of a neurological examination.
A	B	C	D		8. Comedians are given a test of humor to determine if they receive a high score on this trait.

EXERCISE 5-B:
COLLECTING EVALUATION INFORMATION

Directions:

A federally-funded adult education economics program specifically designed for senior citizens is being evaluated by its staff. Several questions have arisen that the staff feel require the help of an evaluator. As the evaluator, please respond to the following questions from the staff. The answers to this exercise can be found on page 34.

Question 1:

We want to involve participants in the program's development and evaluation. Would you advise hiring participants to act as information collectors?

Answer 1:

_____

_____

_____

_____

_____

Question 2:

We are planning a two-hour training session for information collectors. The first hour is spent on the purposes of the program and the information collection activities. During the second hour should trainees practice collecting information, discuss information collection activities, or see the film about information collection that we prepared?

Answer 2:

_____

_____

_____

_____

_____

Question 3:

The primary information collection instrument used will be an achievement test given during the last session of each course. We developed the test ourselves and need to pilot test it to ensure its reliability and validity. We have been considering two groups as participants in the pilot test: undergraduate students majoring in economics at a local community college, who could give substantive comments and students in one of the classes participating in the program, but who will not participate further in the evaluation. Which group would you recommend?

Answer 3:

_____

_____

_____

_____

_____

Question 4:

We plan to have the instructor for each course administer the achievement test during the last class session. For the pilot test we are unsure who should administer the test—the course instructors, the evaluator, or persons who developed the curriculum. Which of these would you recommend?

Answer 4:

_____

_____

_____

_____

_____

Question 5:

In addition to the achievement test, we planned several other information collection activities. These include a course evaluation questionnaire that will be administered at the end of the program and an interview that will be conducted at the time of enrollment. We do not have time to try out the interviews, but we will field test the achievement test and the questionnaire. Do you see any difficulties with this pilot test plan?

Answer 5:

_____

_____

_____

_____

_____

Question 6:

We have decided to clear our questionnaire, interview, and achievement test with a panel of experts who understand the role of instrumentation in federally-funded programs like ours. We have allotted two weeks for the review and another week to make modifications in the instruments based on experts' comments. At the end of the third week, we plan to begin collecting information. Can you anticipate any problems with this plan?

Answer 6:

_____

_____

_____

_____

_____

Question 7:

This summer we are planning to conduct a telephone interview survey to help us identify future topics for our economics program. In order to assure a high response rate, we have attempted to obtain recent telephone listings for each person selected for the survey, and we plan to hire interviewers who can make telephone calls at different times during the day or evening. Is there anything else we can do to produce a high rate of response to our survey?

Answer 7:

_____

_____

_____

_____

_____

Question 8:

The program instructors will administer the achievement test and the course evaluation questionnaire. How can we monitor their information collection efforts?

Answer 8:

_____

_____

_____

_____

_____

Question 9:

We plan to include 50 people in the telephone interview survey and think that we can analyze the data without assistance of a computer. The interview form has been reviewed by a panel of experts who recommended that the responses to the questions be precategorized. Do we also need to assign numerical codes to the responses?

Answer 9:

_____

_____

_____

_____

_____

Question 10:

One of our evaluation questions asks whether the program has more appeal as a learning or a social experience. To answer the question, participants were asked in the course evaluation questionnaire: "What was the best part of the program?" Some of the responses to this question were:
    —I am able to buy things more intelligently
    —Learning about my rights to social security
    —The readings
    —I like to listen to interesting people
    —The lectures
    —The classroom atmosphere
    —Meeting guest lecturers
    —Getting to know the instructor
    —I made new friends
    —Knowledge of medicare and health benefits
    —The discussions were stimulating
    —I enjoyed going to school again
    —Keeping up
    —Everyone was very nice
    —It breaks up the routine
    —They let our entire group take the course together.
Please help us categorize the responses so that we can analyze them.

Answer 10:

_____

_____

_____

_____

_____

Answers to Exercise 5-A: Measurement Validity

Predictive Concurrent Content Construct

Ⓐ B C D   1. At the end of the second year of medical school, students take a battery of tests to find out who will and will not become good doctors.

A Ⓑ C D   2. Teacher's evaluation of the quality of student's writing was correlated with scores obtained on the APC Test of Writing Ability.

A B Ⓒ D   3. Confronted by a frantic student who has just received the results of his/her History 103 test, the teacher discovers that the student in question was given a History 113 test by mistake.

Ⓐ B C D   4. The director of the Center for the Study of Instruction judges which teachers will benefit most from the workshop on how to evaluate educational materials.

A B C Ⓓ   5. Teachers who become angry in an experimental situation also obtain higher anger scores on the new personality measure than do teachers whose anger is not experimentally manipulated.

A B Ⓒ D   6. Confident that the professor has not changed his course, students studied for the final exam by reviewing their fraternity's file of past exams.

A Ⓑ C D   7. A diagnosis of brain damage based on the new XYZ Perceptual Performance Test is compared with the results of a neurological examination.

A B C Ⓓ   8. Comedians are given a test of humor to determine if they receive a high score on this trait.

Answers to Exercise 5-B: Collecting Evaluation Information

Question 1:

We want to involve participants in the program's development and evaluation. Would you advise hiring participants to act as information collectors?

Answer 1:

No. Program participants are likely to be biased information collectors because of their involvement with the program. Also, participants are usually the subjects of an evaluation and therefore should not conduct any of the activities.

Question 2:

We are planning a two-hour training session for information collectors. The first hour is spent on the purposes of the program and the information collection activities. During the second hour should trainees practice collecting information, discuss information collection activities, or see the film about information collection that we prepared?

Answer 2:

All three training techniques sound good. However, only the practice is essential.

Question 3:

The primary information collection instrument used will be an achievement test given during the last session of each course. We developed the test ourselves and need to pilot test it to ensure its reliability and validity. We have been considering two groups as participants in the pilot test: undergraduate students majoring in economics at a local community college, who could give substantive comments and students in one of the classes participating in the program, but who will not participate further in the evaluation. Which group would you recommend?

Answer 3:

It would be best to choose one of the classes participating in the program because they are most representative of the target population for whom the program is intended. The class can be used in the pilot test as long as it is not also included in the evaluation. If more than one group could be included in the pilot test, it might be desirable to have specialists in economics take the test and review it for accuracy and relevance. It would not be a good idea to use only undergraduate students in economics since they are not representative of the target population.

Question 4:

We plan to have the instructor for each course administer the achievement test during the last class session. For the pilot test we are unsure who should administer the test—the course instructors, the evaluator, or persons who developed the curriculum. Which of these would you recommend?

Answer 4:

The course instructors are recommended since they will eventually be responsible for administering the test. The evaluator and developers might want to observe the test administration in order to get a first-hand view of any problems. However, since neither of them will administer the test in practice, they should not administer it in the pilot run.

Question 5:

In addition to the achievement test, we have planned several other information collection activities. These include a course evaluation questionnaire that will be administered at the end of the program and an interview that will be conducted at the time of enrollment. We do not have time to try out the interviews, but we will field test the achievement test and the questionnaire. Do you see any difficulties with this pilot test plan?

Answer 5:

All information collection activities should be pilot tested. Not testing the interviews will cast serious doubt on the information obtained from them. In this situation, the use of interviews might be reconsidered since the outcomes will be of questionable validity.

Question 6:

We have decided to clear our questionnaire, interview, and achievement tests with a panel of experts who understand the role of instrumentation in federally-funded programs like ours. We have allotted two weeks for the review and another week to make modifications in the instruments based on the experts' comments. At the end of the third week, we plan to begin collecting information. Can you anticipate any problems with this plan?

Answer 6:

Because your program is federally funded, you must submit all instruments that will be administered to ten or more people to the Office of Management and Budget for their clearance. This process can take several months, so you may need to adjust your schedule.

Question 7:

This summer we are planning to conduct a telephone interview survey to help us identify future topics for our economics program. In order to assure a high response rate, we have attempted to obtain recent telephone listings for each person selected for the survey, and we plan to hire interviewers who can make telephone calls at different times during the day or evening. Is there anything else we can do to produce a high rate of response to our survey?

Answer 7:

Yes. You can send a letter to the people selected for the survey to inform them of the interview and to request their cooperation.

Question 8:

The program instructors will administer the achievement test and the course evaluation questionnaire. How can we monitor their information collection efforts?

Answer 8:

The evaluation team can observe some or all of the program instructors, or the instructors can be asked to complete a report that describes what information was collected, from whom, and whether any problems were encountered.

Question 9:

We plan to include 50 people in the telephone interview survey and think that we can analyze the data without assistance of a computer. The interview form has been reviewed by a panel of experts who recommended that the responses to the questions be precategorized. Do we also need to assign numerical codes to the responses?

Answer 9:

No. Although they can be a convenient shorthand, numerical codes are necessary only when a computer is being used.

Question 10:

One of our evaluation questions asks whether the program has more appeal as a learning or a social experience. To answer the question, participants were asked in the course evaluation questionnaire: "What was the best part of the program?" Some of the responses to this question were:
—I am able to buy things more intelligently
—Learning about my rights to social security
—The readings
—I like to listen to interesting people
—The lectures
—The classroom atmosphere
—Meeting guest lecturers
—Getting to know the instructor
—I made new friends
—Knowledge of medicare and health benefits
—The discussions were stimulating
—I enjoyed going to school again
—Keeping up
—Everyone was very nice
—It breaks up the routine
—They let our entire group take the course together
Please help us categorize the responses so that we can analyze them.

Answer 10:

Since the evaluation only asks about two aspects of the program, learning and social experience, establish two categories that are congruent with them and perhaps add a third category for responses that cannot be categorized as either a learning or social experience. Under the category of learning experience should fall:

—The lectures
—I am able to buy things more intelligently
—The discussions were stimulating
—Learning about my rights to social security
—Knowledge of medicare and other health benefits
—The readings

Under the category of social experience would fall:

—Getting to know the instructor
—I made new friends
—Meeting guest lecturers
—I enjoyed going to school again
—The classroom atmosphere
—It breaks up the routine
—They let our group take the course together
—Everyone was very nice

Under the "not sure" category would fall:

—Keeping current
—I like to listen to interesting people

CHAPTER 6
PLANNING AND CONDUCTING INFORMATION ANALYSIS ACTIVITIES

EXERCISE 6-A:
INTERPRETING EVALUATION INFORMATION

Directions:

In this exercise you will evaluate a physical education program in which boys and girls participate together. It involves sports like tennis, baseball, dance, gymnastics, and badminton.

On the following pages you are given two evaluation questions, their matching information analysis methods, and portions of the analysis results. For each evaluation question there are also four alternative interpretations. Select the interpretation that makes the best use of the analysis results and that provides the appropriate answer to the evaluation question.

The answers to this exercise are on page 44.

Evaluation Question #1: According to students, which sport was most enjoyable?

- -

INFORMATION ANALYSIS METHOD

Descriptive statistics using information from questionnaires and interview surveys to compute mean ratings for each sport

- -

PORTION OF INFORMATION ANALYSIS RESULTS

Ratings of Sports*

Sports	Boys	Girls	Total
Tennis	4.5	3.9	4.2
Baseball	2.0	4.0	3.0
Dance	1.1	3.3	2.1
Gymnastics	1.6	2.0	1.8
Badminton	2.1	0.9	1.5

----
*Rating Scale:
   1 = Least Enjoyable; 5 = Most Enjoyable

(continued)

INTERPRETATIONS

(Select One)

A. The most enjoyable sport was tennis. This sport was selected because most students like net games.
B. The sport considered most enjoyable by boys was tennis. The sport considered most enjoyable by girls was baseball. However, girls felt less strongly than boys about this issue.
C. Boys overwhelmingly considered tennis as more enjoyable than the other sports.
D. The sport considered to be most enjoyable was tennis.

Evaluation Question #2: Is there a difference in the sports activities requested by boys and girls?

INFORMATION ANALYSIS METHODS

Descriptive Statistics: tally of the information from a record review

PORTIONS OF INFORMATION ANALYSIS RESULTS

Number of Sports Activities Requested

Sports	Boys	Girls
Tennis	145	89
Baseball	90	99
Dance	75	102
Gymnastics	17	25
Badminton	82	94
Total Number of Requests	409	409

INTERPRETATIONS

(Select One)

A. There are no differences in the total number of sports activities requested by boys and girls, although more boys request tennis than girls.
B. There are differences in the sports activities requested by boys and girls, with boys requesting tennis most often and girls requesting dance most often.
C. There are no differences in the sports activities requested by boys and girls, with both requesting about the same total number of sports activities.
D. There are differences in the sports activities requested by boys and girls. Boys requested tennis but girls did not, and girls requested dance but boys did not.

EXERCISE 6-B:
PREPARING AN INFORMATION ANALYSIS PLAN
Directions:

Prepare an Information Analysis Plan (IAP) for the program described below using the form provided for this purpose. The answers to this exercise are on page 45.

Program Description

General Relativity is a four-week unit for gifted high school students that is part of their physics program. Its purpose is to introduce students to Einstein's general theory of relativity, and in particular to the concepts of the equivalence of mass and energy and space-time dilations. At the beginning of the unit students are given an achievement test, and at the end they are given a parallel achievement test and a questionnaire asking for their reactions to the unit. In addition, teachers are asked to complete a questionnaire that asks for their reactions to the unit.

Information Analysis Plan

Evaluation Questions	Description of the Design	Source of the Information	Analysis Method	Limitations
1. Has there been a statistically significant increase in students' knowledge of relativity?				
2. Did boys and girls differ in their enjoyment of the unit?				
3. What aspects of the unit did they like best?				

EXERCISE 6-C:
ANSWERING EVALUATION QUESTIONS

Directions:

You are given either raw data or the results of analyses conducted for an evaluation of the General Relativity unit for gifted high school students. Analyze the data and interpret the results to answer the evaluation questions.

The answers to this exercise are on page 46.

Evaluation Question 1: Has there been a statistically significant increase in students' knowledge of relativity?

Instructions: Below are the raw data from the pretest and posttest of the General Relativity Achievement Test. The test has 20 questions and the highest possible score is 20 points. Analyze the data and interpret the results.

DATA

Students' ID	Pretest Scores	Posttest Scores
001	00	06
002	00	08
003	01	10
004	01	03
005	01	11
006	02	12
007	02	09
008	02	07
009	02	04
010	03	10
011	03	13
012	03	14
013	03	14
014	04	11
015	04	08
016	04	12
017	04	13
018	04	10
019	05	04
020	05	07
021	05	09
022	05	14
023	05	11
024	06	08
025	06	14
026	06	15
027	06	16
028	06	11
029	06	08
030	07	07
031	07	10
032	07	12
033	07	13
034	07	15
035	07	13

Students' ID	Pretest Scores	Posttest Scores
036	07	11
037	07	04
038	07	08
039	07	16
040	08	17
041	08	17
042	08	15
043	08	15
044	08	13
045	08	09
046	08	10
047	08	14
048	08	16
049	08	15
050	08	13
051	08	10
052	08	09
053	09	09
054	09	11
055	09	16
056	09	17
057	09	15
058	09	13
059	09	14
060	09	16
061	09	18
062	09	18
063	09	17
064	09	07
065	09	18
066	09	17
067	09	17
068	09	15
069	09	13
070	09	14
071	09	17
072	10	15
073	10	18
074	10	19
075	10	17
076	10	15
077	10	19
078	10	17
079	10	18
080	10	17
081	10	19
082	10	20
083	10	19
084	11	18
085	11	15
086	11	17
087	11	19
088	11	19

089	11	17
090	11	19
091	11	19
092	11	18
093	11	18
094	11	18
095	12	15
096	12	17
097	12	17
098	12	19
099	12	18
100	12	19
101	13	18
102	13	19
103	13	17
104	13	19
105	13	18
106	14	18
107	14	18
108	14	17
109	14	19
110	14	18
111	15	20
112	15	20
113	15	17
114	15	19
115	16	18
116	16	20
117	16	20
118	16	18
119	17	19
120	17	19
121	17	19
122	18	18
123	18	19
124	19	18
125	19	19
126	20	20

Use this space for computations.

Interpretation:

_____

_____

_____

_____

_____

_____

Evaluation Question 2: Did boys and girls differ in their enjoyment of the unit?

Instructions: Interpret the following results:

Table XX: Results of a Chi Square Test

Question 5 from Student
    Questionnaire:
Did you like this unit on
relativity?

	Boys	Girls	Totals
Yes, Very Much	38	41	79
Yes, Somewhat	39	32	71
No, Not Very Much	37	37	74
No, Not At All	43	40	83
Totals	157	150	307

X^2 = Chi square = .7532
df = 3

Interpretation:

_____

_____

_____

_____

_____

Answers to Exercise 6-A: Interpreting Evaluation Information

Evaluation Question #1: According to students, which sport was most enjoyable?

SELECTED INTERPRETATION

Interpretation D is most appropriate.

Interpretation A is incorrect because the evaluator has no way of knowing from the information provided why tennis was considered most enjoyable.

Interpretation B is incorrect because it does not directly answer the evaluation question. The combined answer for boys and girls was not reported and should have been.

Interpretation C is incorrect because it does not directly answer the evaluation question. The sport that was considered most enjoyable by boys and girls together should have been reported.

Evaluation Question #2: Is there a difference in the sports activities requested by boys and girls?

SELECTED INTERPRETATION

Interpretation B is most appropriate.

Interpretation A is incorrect because there <u>is</u> a difference in the sports activities requested by boys and girls. Information about the total <u>number</u> of sports activities requested is not called for by the evaluation question.

Interpretation C is incorrect. There <u>is</u> a difference in the sports activities requested.

Interpretation D is incorrect because some boys do request dance and some girls do request tennis.

Answers to Exercise 6-B: Preparing an Information Analysis Plan

Information Analysis Plan

Evaluation Questions	Description of the Design	Source of the Information	Analysis Methods	Limitations
1. Has there been a statistically significant increase in students' knowledge of relativity?	*Pre* | *Post* *Independent variable: Timing of measures* *Dependent variable: Knowledge of relativity*	*Pre- and post-instruction achievement tests*	*Dependent t-test or one-way repeated-measures ANOVA*	*May lose data from students who did not complete the pre- and post-instruction achievement tests*
2. Did boys and girls differ in their enjoyment of the unit?	*Boys | Girls* *Not at All* *Some-what* *Very Much*	*Student question-naire*	*Chi square comparing the frequency of boys' and girls' responses to the relevant questions*	*Students may evaluate their teachers and not the unit (a halo effect)*
3. What aspects of the unit did they like best?	*Participants in the Unit* *Independent variable: Participation in the unit* *Dependent variable: Characteristics of the unit*	*Student question-naire* *Teacher question-naire*	*Descriptive statistics*	*Students may evaluate their teachers and not the unit (a halo effect)*

Answers to Exercise 6-C: Answering Evaluation Questions

Evaluation Findings

Evaluation Question 1: Has there been a statistically significant increase in students' knowledge of relativity?

A dependent t-test was conducted to determine whether students' knowledge of relativity increased as a result of their participation in the program. The independent variable was time of testing, which was investigated at two levels: pre- and post-instruction. The dependent variable was students' knowledge as represented by scores on the General Relativity Achievement Test. The hypotheses being tested in the analysis were:

   Null hypothesis: Pretest mean score = Posttest mean score
   Alternate hypothesis: Pretest mean score < Posttest mean score
The results of the analysis are given in Table X.

Table X: Results of a Dependent t-Test

Time of Testing	Mean * Score	Standard Deviation	Number of Cases	Corre- lation	t-Value	Degrees of Freedom	One-Tailed Significance
Preinstruction	9.25	4.32					
			126	.75	20.38	125	<.01
Postinstruction	14.72	4.26					

*Total possible score on Test = 20 points

As can be seen from Table X, the t-value is significant, indicating that students' increase in knowledge was statistically meaningful. Thus the answer to Evaluation Question 1 is yes.

Evaluation Question 2: Did boys and girls differ in their enjoyment of the unit?

A contingency table analysis using the chi square statistic was conducted to find out whether there was a relationship between the sex of the students and their enjoyment of the unit. The variables included in the analysis were students' sex and their responses to a question asking if they liked the unit on relativity. The results of the analysis are given in Table XX.

Table XX: Results of a Chi Square Test

Question 5 from Student Questionnaire: Did you like this unit on relativity?

Responses to Question 5	Boys	Girls	Totals
Yes, Very Much	38	41	79
Yes, Somewhat	39	32	71
No, Not Very Much	37	37	74
No, Not At All	43	40	83
Totals	157	150	307

X^2 = Chi square = .7532
df = 3

The obtained chi square value of .7532 was less than the corresponding value in the Chi square table, indicating there is no relationship between students' sex and enjoyment of the unit. This suggests that the answer to Evaluation Question 2 is no.

CHAPTER 7
REPORTING EVALUATION INFORMATION

Exercise 7-A:
Writing Evaluation Reports

Directions:

In this exercise, you will describe some limitations on an evaluation of the comparative effectiveness of three federally-funded education programs, describe evaluation results, and answer an evaluation question. Summaries of parts of some chapters of an evaluation report are given to help you do the exercise. Use only the information that is provided when you write the report.

The answers to this exercise are on page 50.

Portions of Summaries of Evaluation Reports	Task to be Completed
Chapter 1: INTRODUCTION TO THE EVALUATION	
Evaluation Question: What are the differences among the X, Y, and Z programs with respect to program costs, students' achievement and attitudes, and staff attitudes?	No task is to be completed.
Chapter 3: INFORMATION COLLECTION	
Students in each of the three programs were: 1) tested every month using criterion-referenced tests; 2) required to keep a diary of their progress; 3) interviewed by a member of the evaluation team in May. Twice a year an auditor examined the financial records for each program. The participants in the evaluation were students who received low scores on either a verbal or quantitative achievement test. Students were assigned to one of the programs by their counselor.	Describe the limitations caused by the sampling plan.

Chapter 6: ANALYSIS

At the end of a year, the programs were compared with respect to student achievement and attitudes, staff attitudes, and costs. Student achievement was reported on a scale of 1 to 100, with 100 being a perfect score and 50 being the average score for a student in the state. Staff and student attitudes to the program were reported on a five-point scale, with 5 being very good and 1 being very poor. Yearly costs were reported per student for each item on the budget.

The following table summarizes the results of the analysis:

	Program X	Program Y	Program Z
Student Achievement			
Average Score	65	65	65
Range	32-85	28–72	41–87
Sample Size	53	42	49
Student Attitudes			
Average Score	4.2	3.0	3.2
Range	2–5	1–5	1–5
Sample Size	53	42	49
Staff Attitudes			
Average Score	2.1	3.2	4.2
Range	1–4	1–5	3–5
Sample Size	11	15	18
Average Yearly Costs Per Student	$310	$352	$409

Describe the results for Program Y.

Chapter 8: EVALUATION FINDINGS

Evaluation Question: What are the differences among the X, Y, and Z programs with respect to program costs, students' achievement and attitudes, and staff attitudes?

Answer the evaluation question, and give at least one recommendation based on the findings.

Use this space for calculations.

Use this space for calculations.

Answers to 7-A:
Writing Evaluation Reports

Portions of Summaries of Evaluation Reports	Task to be Completed
Chapter 1: INTRODUCTION TO THE EVALUATION Evaluation Question: What are the differences among the X, Y, and Z programs with respect to program costs, students' achievement and attitudes, and staff attitudes?	No task is to be completed.
Chapter 3: INFORMATION COLLECTION Students in each of the three programs were: 1) tested every month using criterion-referenced tests; 2) required to keep a diary of their progress; 3)interviewed by a member of the evaluation team in May. Twice a year an auditor examined the financial records for each program. The participants in the evaluation were students who received low scores on either a verbal or quantitative achievement test. Students were assigned to one of the programs by their counselor.	Describe the limitations caused by the sampling plan. *Students may be quite different in terms of their background or learning difficulties. Further, because the students are not necessarily representative of all students in the state, the results are probably not generalizable.*

Chapter 6: ANALYSIS

At the end of a year, the programs were compared with respect to students' achievement and attitudes, staff attitudes, and costs. Student achievement was reported on a scale of 1 to 100, with 100 being a perfect score and 50 being the average score for a student in the state. Staff and student attitudes to the program were reported on a five-point scale, with 5 being very good and 1 being very poor. Yearly costs were reported per student for each item on the budget. The results of the analysis were summarized in a table as follows:

	Program X	Program Y	Program Z
Student Achievement			
Average Score	65	65	65
Range	52-85	28-72	41-87
Sample Size	53	42	49
Student Attitudes			
Average Score	4.2	3.0	3.2
Range	2-5	1-5	1-5
Sample Size	53	42	49
Staff Attitudes			
Average Score	2.1	3.2	4.2
Range	1-4	1-5	3-5
Sample Size	11	15	18
Average Yearly Costs per Student	$310	$352	$409

Describe the results for Program Y

Based on a sample of 42, student achievement at the end of a year is clearly above the state average of 50, with a mean score of 65 points and a range of 28-72 points. Student attitudes are fair with an average score of 3 points and a range of 1-5 points. Based on a sample of 15, staff attitudes are also fair with an average score of 3.2 points and a range of 1-5 points. The annual average costs of the program amount to $352 for each student.

Chapter 8: EVALUATION FINDINGS

Evaluation Question: What are the differences among the X, Y, and Z programs with respect to program costs, students' achievement and attitudes, and staff attitudes?	Answer the evaluation question, and give at least one recommendation based on the findings. *Program X is the most economical ($310 per student per year), followed by Program Y ($352), and Program Z ($409).* *The achievement of students in all three programs is very good, with an average score of 65 points, although Program Z has fewer very low scores.* *Student attitudes are best in Program X (4.2) followed by Program Z (3.2).* *Staff attitudes are best in Program Z (4.2), followed by Program Y (3.2).* *Recommendations: The poor attitudes of the staff in Program X may be related to the relatively small size of the staff. The evaluator recommends an investigation of this possibility.*

CHAPTER 8
MANAGING AN EVALUATION

EXERCISE 8-A:
PREPARING AN EVALUATION MANAGEMENT PLAN

Directions:

The school district has commissioned an effectiveness evaluation of a two-year-old program, the Neighborhood Garden Program, in which classrooms use 1/12 acre of city land to grow fruits and vegetables for their own consumption. As the director of the evaluation, you are to complete a management plan by assigning your staff to specific evaluation activities. To do this, you are given:

- a list of the evaluation staff and the number of days each person has available for each activity
- a time line showing the beginning and ending days and total number of days allocated for each activity
- a partially completed management plan which includes a list of seven evaluation activities, the beginning and ending days and total number of days allocated for each.

You must decide which staff members will be involved in each activity (based on their skills) and how many of their total available days each person will spend on a given activity.

The answers to this exercise are on page 56.

Staff for the Three-Month Evaluation of the Neighborhood Garden Program

Title	Time Available
Evaluation Director	60 days (100%)
Field Coordinator (Information Collection)	30 days (50%)
Information Analyst	15 days (25%)
Instrument Expert	10 days (16 2/3%)

Time Line

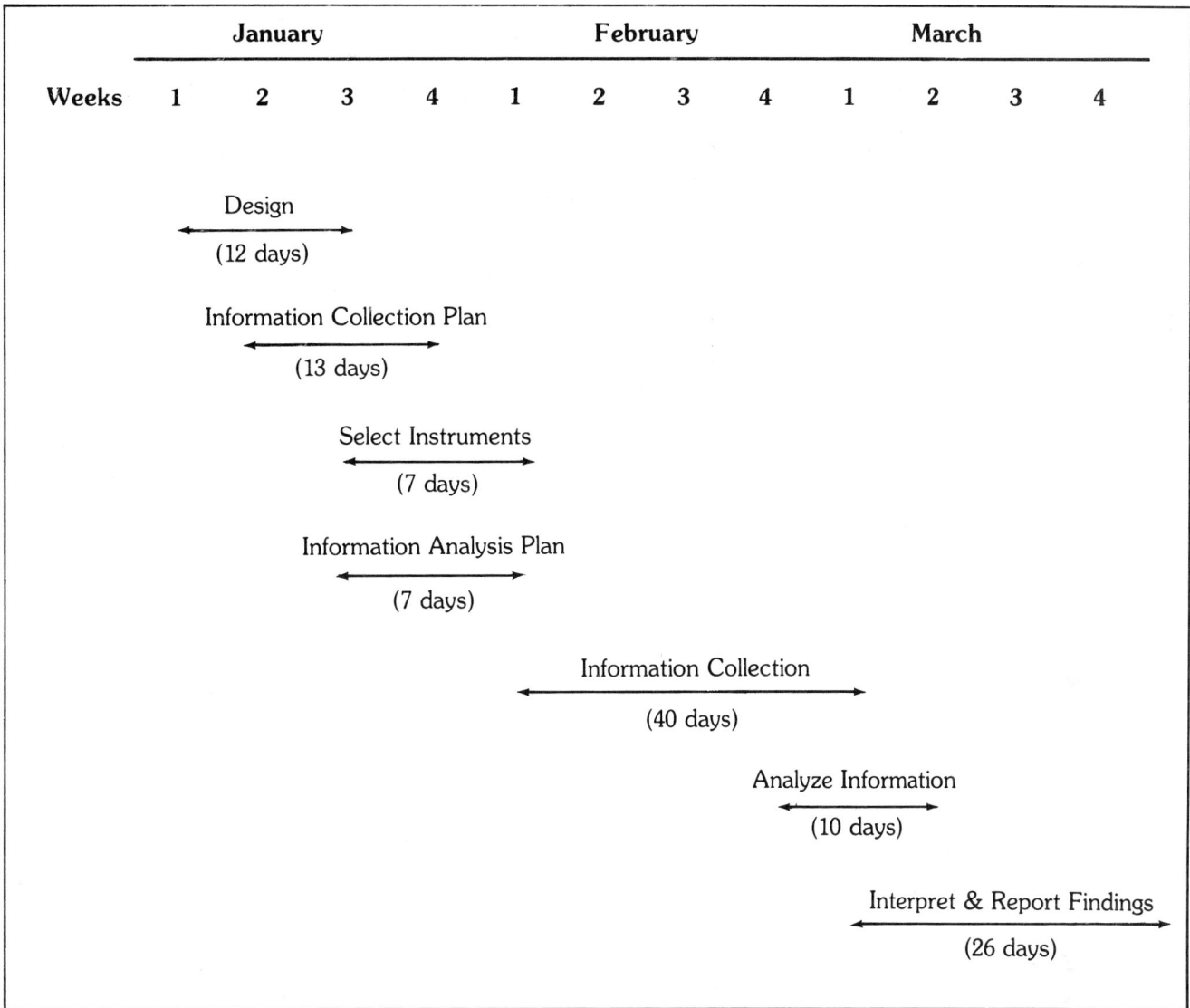

Management Plan for Neighborhood Garden Evaluation

Evaluation Activities	Dates		Staff Assignments	Time Allocation (in days)	
	Beginning	Ending		By Staff Member	Total
1. Develop the design strategy and sampling plan	January 1	January 15			
2. Prepare information collection plan	January 8	January 22			
3. Select instruments	January 16	January 31			
4. Prepare information analysis plan	January 16	January 31			
5. Collect information	February 1	February 28			
6. Analyze information		March 7			
7. Interpret and report evaluation findings	March 1	March 30			

EXERCISE 8-B:
PREPARING AN EVALUATION BUDGET

Directions:

Prepare a budget for the evaluation of the Neighborhood Garden Program using the information given below.

Information Needed to Complete Budget

Duration of the Evaluation: January 1 - March 31
Cost of the Total Evaluation: Not to exceed $20,000
Personnel Titles, Time Allotments, and Annual Salaries:

Title	Time	Annual Salaries
Evaluation Director	100%	$ 24,000
Field Coordinator	50%	17,000
Information Analyst	25%	20,000
Instrument Expert	16 2/3%	25,000

Budget Items:

Salaries and Wages
Benefits (16% of Salaries and Wages)
Rent
Office Supplies
Equipment
Computer
Telephone and Mail
Printing and Reproduction
Travel
Indirect Costs (30% of Salaries and Wages)

The answers to this exercise are on page 57.

Answers to Exercise 8-A:
Preparing an Evaluation Management Plan
Management Plan for Neighborhood Garden Evaluation

Evaluation Activities	Dates		Staff Assignments	Time Allocation (in days)	
	Beginning	Ending		By Staff Member	Total
1. Developing the design strategy and sampling plan	January 1	January 15	Evaluation Director Field Coordinator Information Analyst Instrument Expert	8 2 1 1	12
2. Prepare information collection plan	January 8	January 22	Evaluation Director Field Coordinator	7 3 1 2	13
3. Select instruments	January 16	January 31	Evaluation Director Information Analyst Instrument Expert	2 1 4	7
4. Prepare information analysis plan	January 16	January 31	Evaluation Director Information Analyst Instrument Expert	3 3 1	7
5. Collect information	February 1	February 28	Evaluation Director Field Coordinator	20 20	40
6. Analyze information	February 21	March 7	Evaluation Director Information Analyst	5 5	10
7. Interpret and report evaluation findings	March 1	March 30	Evaluation Director Field Coordinator Information Analyst Instrument Expert	15 5 4 2	26

Answers to Exercise 8-B: Preparing an Evaluation Budget

DIRECT COSTS

I. STAFF

A. Salaries and Wages

1. Evaluation Director at $24,000 per annum .... $ 6,000
   100% for 3 months
2. Field Coordinator at $17,000 per annum 2,125
   50% for 3 months
3. Information Analyst at $20,000 per annum... 1,250
   25% for 3 months
4. Instrument Expert at $25,000 per annum 1,042
   16 2/3% for 3 months
                                                                                    _____

                                                                                    $10,417

B. Employee Benefits

   16% of Salaries and Wages ($10,417) 1,667

II. NON-STAFF

A. Rent

1. Office space and maintenance at $150 450
   per month for 3 months

B. Office Supplies

1. Stationery, etc. at $50 per month for 150
   3 months

C. Equipment

1. Rental of photocopy machine, typewriter, ... 150
   etc. at $50 per month for 3 months

D. Computer

1. Computer Time 400
2. Data processing supplies (cards, keypunching) 350

E. Telephone and Mail

1. Telephone at $25 per month for 3 months 75
2. Postage at $10 per month for 3 months 30

F. Printing and Reproduction

1. Printing questionnaires and reports 270

G. Travel

1. Local Travel, 200 miles at 15¢ per mile 30
                                                                                    _____

	Subtotal Direct Costs	$13,989

INDIRECT COSTS

30% of Salaries and Wages ($10,417) 3,125

	Subtotal Indirect Costs	$ 3,125

GRAND TOTAL $17,114